Alive for the

JOURNEY

LAEL PUBLISHING

Author: Brenda A. Kearney
Published by Lael Publishing, LLC
Winston Salem, North Carolina
www.LaelAgency.com

ISBN 978-1-954433-13-7

Dedication

I am a proud auntie of countless biological and non-biological nieces, nephews, and other children around the world; I am also an honored godmother of twelve. I dedicate this, my first book, to all of you with all my love, and ask you to remember two things:

First, "seek the kingdom of God above all else, and live righteously, and He will give you everything you need." (Matthew 6:33 NLT)

And, "Delight thyself also in the Lord; And he shall give thee the desires of thine heart." (Psalm 37:4 KJV)

Comments from my godchildren, children of the world, and their parents:

"Happy birthday to the best Godmother in the land."

"You always inspire me spiritually."

"Because you feel like an extended mother to me. Happy Mother's Day."

"Happy Mother's Day! We've only known each other for a few months. But you have cared for me as a mother would. I find a little peace and joy simply because you are part of my life. Today I honor and thank you."

"I adopted you as my mother many years ago."

"Thank you for teaching and imparting to my kids. You are one we trust, and our kids trust and love you."

"I know God will use you to help us raise our child right and impart spiritual values."

Acknowledgements

Thank you, girlfriends from coast to coast, who irritated and inspired me often by asking "How is the book writing progressing?" It wasn't progressing when you asked, because I had not started it yet. But because of your consistent perseverance in asking me, I finally started writing and now the book is finished. Thank you, genuine sisters.

Thank you to my nieces and nephews for inspiring me to leave a legacy to you. This is just the beginning of your legacy from me. Remember I am, and you are, alive for the Journey that God has for us. Don't delay!

To my extended Florida family- the next time we have dinner, it will be true when you say, "I am eating dinner with an author." Thank you for your encouragement and for speaking those things that didn't exist at the time. You spoke life to this book.

Family and friends, near and far, thank you for being there for me in times I needed you the most, both good and bad! Family matters!

Thanks to my mentors and co-laborers in the gospel. Thanks for teaching and demonstrating God's love. You've been mighty in prayer, and pastors of faith without wavering.

Your ministries have made an eternal impact on my life.

Thank you to Bishop James C. & Mrs. Joyce Hash, Sr., Pastors of St. Peter's Church & World Outreach Center, Winston-Salem, North Carolina, for being devoted spiritual parents, pastors, and great employers. You have taught, inspired, and covered me in prayer while showing compassion and love. God has used your faith-walk to increase my faith in His Word.

To Dr. Larry & LaVonna Cockerham, Cleveland, TN, thank you for exposing me to the world of missions. You believed in me, trained, covered me as your own and took me on my first of many mission trips. Your mentorship and love made a difference.

Other impactful spiritual leaders along my journey have included:

-Bishop John McClurklin & the late Missionary Janice McClurklin, Winston-Salem, NC

-Drs. Gehazel & Viola Williams, Aiken, SC

-Mother Mary Quick & the late Elder James Quick, Cincinnati, OH

-Rev. Pearl Mangum & the late Pastor David Mangum, Richland, WA

-The late Bishop Willie & Mother Minnie Vaughn, Seattle, Washington

-The late Pastor Dennis Wooten, Roanoke Rapids, NC

-Mother Annie P. Moody, Jurisdictional Supervisor, C.O.G.I.C. (South Carolina) Aiken, SC

-Dr. Patricia Bailey, Patricia Bailey Ministries

-The late Pastor Burnice Kearney & Rev. Fannie Kearney Johnson, Parents, Warrenton, NC

-The late Mr. Willie Johnson, stepfather, Warrenton, NC

Influence from teachers has also been central to my experience. These teachers encouraged and empowered me to excel academically: I will forever cherish Mrs. Eunice Bell Evans and the late Mrs. Lillian Martin.

And finally, I want to thank those who helped me start this writing process, even if they did not realize they were doing so. When it was my first time to begin this work, I met an agent/ghost writer who was excited to help me fulfill it. But as we talked, within the first five minutes or so she said "I don't write God books. If your book is all about God, I can't write it." I meditated on what she said overnight, then the next day I called her back to thank her, but I could not compromise my faith and vision by utilizing her service.

Within an hour of that call, I learned, through a friend, about The Lael Agency, drawing from the Hebrew word "Lael" that means "Of God." I knew then that I had the right agency, and this was confirmed when the Lael representative I spoke with said, "Someone tried to exclude God from your story, but God is your story."

Endorsements

"Alive For The Journey" is a wealth of challenging experiences from first time author, Brenda A. Kearney, overcoming seemingly insurmountable obstacles. Each hurdle she overcame was a testament to her inner strength, resilience and faith which moved her forward on her journey. The author discovered strengths she didn't know she possessed and uncovered new aspects of her identity.

We were greatly impacted by our spiritual daughter's unwavering faith in God. She encouraged herself and others while embracing life's uncertainties with courage. This book is a must-read for anyone passionate about overcoming obstacles. As long as you have breath, hope, and faith "there is nothing impossible with God."

Bishop James C. & Mrs. Joyce Hash, Senior Pastors
St. Peter's Church & World Outreach Center

"We are blessed to write a brief endorsement for our dear friend and beloved spiritual daughter, Brenda A. Kearney. She is a true woman of God and a woman of excellence in every way. She has visited in our home, ministered in our church and traveled with us on international missions trips. She exemplifies whole-hearted devotion to God and to the ministry. We join the body of Christ all over the world in welcoming this beautiful new book. We believe this book will be a blessing to thousands of people all over the world."

Dr. Larry Cockerham
President, International Ministries Network

LaVonna Cockerham
Director, Cleveland Net

"I highly recommend this remarkable and amazing book. It is full of important information for those of us who have been through multiple valley experiences. My life was transformed reading it. This author tells about her incredible mustard seed of faith. This book is a must-read for anyone facing challenges in different areas of life and overcoming them."

Vivian Barnette, Ph.D., ABPP
Licensed Psychologist

Contents

Chapter 1

Am I Good Enough?

Imagine this. I am in junior high school at 6:00 pm weekly basketball practice. I am on third string, which means I would rarely, if ever, get to play. If anyone walked into the gym and saw the girls' team, you would probably think I was definitely the "water girl," not a team member. You might say, "What is she doing here?"

Well. I was watching, waiting, and wanting. And although I did not know it at the time, a major lesson about life was waiting for me there.

Many times, at basketball practice, I *watched* others practice and play with envy inside, but a smile and joyful clapping on the outside. Looking back, I imagine I portrayed great team spirit with words and actions, but there was a very different story happening on the inside. Did I envy their height, which was probably part of their genes? (Which would seem the obvious reason, since I was small in stature.) Did I really think it was their genes that got them on first and second string, or was it the system of who you know and who knows you? Could I accept the fact that maybe I was not good enough and it did not have anything to do with my height?

Even then, I knew the disjuncture between outside and inside was trying to tell me something, but still, it all came down to *watching*. For a brief period, I refocused to just being happy to be on the team with these other awesome girls, regardless of my position on third string. I started looking forward to going to practice once a week and enjoying the camaraderie, where I would *watch* the coach walk to the edge of the floor, sound the whistle, and point to a team member to run on to the floor to practice on first string, preparing for game day.

When I returned home from practice, my mom would usually ask me, "How was your day and how was practice?" Most days, I would keep it bland, tell her I had fun. But one day I decided to be honest, and I told her, "I want to be a starter on the team. I don't want to be on third string, where I never really get to play."

Mom must have understood there was a deep pain there, a hurt she could not heal. Today, I no longer remember the exact words she *said* to me when I told her this, but I will never forget what she *did*. With the look of her piercing eyes, together with a comforting nod and her thoughtful listening ears, I felt I had the answer – not by what she said, but what she did not say.

What did my mom do in times of disappointment? She *watched* for what was needed, she *waited* on no one to change things for her, and she *wanted* the very best for her beloved ones.

My mom was a woman of great faith who faced many unbearable challenges at a young age, many of which required immediate attention and a sudden lifestyle change. She was widowed at the age of thirty-four and left with seven children to raise alone; those children ranged in age from just 11 months old to 13 years old. My dad was 35 years of age when he left home to go to church one night with my dearest mom, and adored aunt & uncle, and he never returned. He had a stroke that night and died the next day. One of the saddest parts of that whole story is before this tragedy, my mom had never worked. She was a stay-at-home mom. But, in the span of a single day, her whole world was turned upside down. She became the family's only breadwinner, just like that.

Now, back to the basketball story of watching, waiting and wanting change. Seeing my mother's quiet and thoughtful reaction, my mind began to reflect on testimonies I heard frequently in the small Pentecostal Church our family attended at the time. I remembered some of the church members talking about how they fasted for the healing of certain illnesses, then God healed them. In other cases, they fasted for their children to be saved, then God saved some of them. I can imagine at the time I thought, "Why didn't God save all of them?" I have seen examples of God's miracles even in my own life. I actually remember one Christmas when my mom had surgery. She should have been off from work to recover for 6 to 8 weeks, but she returned to work in just 2 weeks. In her own words, "I had children at home, and I had to feed y'all." Oh, what sacrificial love for the sake of your children! And in that same week, someone delivered a lot of food and toys to our house for our Christmas! I believe it happened because of my mom's frequent fasting and praying.

So, as you can see, I had a strong Christian foundation as a child. I believed that if God could heal sickness, save parents' children, and send food to my mom's house for Christmas, then surely, He could prick the coach's heart to elevate me all the way to first string, skipping even second string. I believed God!

So, one day after our weekly game, which I think was on a Wednesday, I had a conversation with Jesus. I simply said, "Jesus, I want to play the first string, and I am going to do a complete fast for 24 hours without water and food." At the tender young age of probably 12 or 13 years old, I was just doing what I had witnessed come true in the older saints around me.

I completed that fast the day before our next practice, which I think was on a Monday. In my heart, I truly believed in practice I was going to witness a miracle. I would hear the whistle and then the coach would say, "Go on the floor, Brenda." Well, during practice the whistle blew for someone else, not for me. So, at first it seemed like it hadn't happened as I hoped and believed. As usual, I still practiced on third string the day before our weekly game.

Then came game day, Wednesday, the day when all would be told. As the game was getting ready to start, there I stood behind one of the team's taller girls, anxious and nervous, waiting to see if God had answered my prayer.

The coach blew the whistle like usual and pointed out four girls to run out on the floor. Then he looked at the fifth girl who usually started, but his eyes passed over her and suddenly he was looking at me. He pointed to me saying, "Brenda, you are starting, go to the floor."

Look at God. He answered my prayer.

Now, I remember sharing with someone this story of how Jesus answered my prayer. At the time, I had a complicated relationship with my faith and my ability to trust in God, which this person knew. So, his response was "If you were not a confessing Christian, then God didn't answer your prayer because He doesn't hear the prayers of non-believers."

Well, my experience had shown that just wasn't true. My response to this person – and it was a little sharp, I can admit – was, "Christian or not, the one thing I know: He answered my prayer, and I played first string."

Little did I know at the time this was the beginning

of a faith journey to believe with God; to know that all things are possible, without limitations.

- I believed the possibilities - that nothing was impossible.
- I refused defeat - I would not allow my mind to minimize what God could do, despite my physical size and never having played first string before.
- I expected the expected - I had already prayed and fasted; therefore, I expected that God would do it.
- I navigated - through the Word of God, fasting, and praying.

This little journey was a defining moment of realizing and knowing what God has for me, that gift is intended for me and no human on earth can hinder it. I learned, through the wondrous miracle which happened for a young girl's basketball game, that I do not have to accept what others say, for it is God who has the final word. My deliverance in something that mattered to me took place because of prayer, fasting, and my mother interceding for me, not in words but by action.

What is even more wondrous is this journey from my girlhood has been reflected in so many places, so many versions, all throughout my life. From then to now, prayer, fasting, and intercession have become a part of who I am. This is my identity. What I didn't know then is how the three would play a tremendous and integral part in my calling and life.

Today, because of prayer, fasting, and intercession, I am "Alive for the Journey." This journey has taken me from rejection to acceptance, from abandonment to forgiveness, sickness to healing, defeats to victories, near death to abundant life, childlessness to birthing spiritual children around the world, and the list goes on.

This book is a brief account of my journey thus far, as well as some of the many experiences-both sad and wondrous that have happened along the way.

I hope by reading this testimony, and by seeing how I have watched, waited, and wanted, you too will be inspired to see the Hand of God in your own life, and to seek what He has for you.

Reflection

1. What is the difference between "noticing" and "waiting?"

2. How did your desire change while you were waiting?

3. Discuss a time when the answered prayer was not in His plan.

Chapter 2

Others Matter Too

One time, I read the definition of "intercession". I took away that, in the dictionary sense, this word means to pray for others. This seems simple and easy, right? But my spirit still felt that something was missing, and there was more to intercession. In fact, my spirit reminded me of a line from a popular song by The Rolling Stones, *I Can't Get No Satisfaction*. You likely know it, the one that goes on by saying, "Cause I try, and I try, and I try, and I try, I can't get no."

Well, reading about intercession for the first

time, I was like that song: not satisfied, needing more explanation. I wrestled with the thought that there has got to be more.

Looking back on that early confusion, my mind offers this memory of an experience that helped me understand. I remember going on an adventure ride with a friend in a nice sports car. We were flying through the mountains, going on my first deep sea fishing trip in Washington state. It was kind of a fraught trip, enjoyable because I was with someone that I liked a lot. But at the same time, it was a little hard because deep down in my soul I knew that he did not like me the way I really liked him. Still, the trip was enjoyable until, while we were driving, I reflected on a true story I heard of just prior. Several teens had been killed in a single car accident, and the newspaper stated that they were driving fast and drunk. Various types of drugs were found in the crashed car.

So, as we drove faster and faster around those winding mountains, I realized I was laughing and listening to R&B music with a boy who I knew didn't really love me. I could not have any peace because my mind was fixated on that tragic car accident with those teens, and I did not want the same thing to happen to me. I began to pray fervently, "Lord, do not let me die now in this car, flying around these curves, so my mom back in North Carolina receives the report that harmful drugs were in my system."

I was so afraid. I did not want to die that way because I knew it would have destroyed my momma. Looking back now, the younger me was more concerned about my body than my soul. I was consumed with the fact that I did not want to hurt my momma, even more than I was concerned about where I would spend eternity if I died there. At the time, I did not know the scripture that tells us, "But rather fear him which is able to destroy both soul and body in hell." (Matthew 10:28 KJV).

When I was that age, my mom would often tell me, "I am praying for you." And even then, I always felt that if momma was praying for me, then everything will be all right. Today, I realize her praying for me was intercessory, which is prayer you pray on behalf of others – asking God to reach forth His Hand not for you, but for a loved one, or someone who is suffering, bringing them His gifts. So now when I think about it, I realize it probably wasn't me and my selfish prayers for the safety of my own body that brought us safely around those mountain roads to our deep-sea fishing destination.

No, it was my mother's fervent prayers that interceded with God for me.

This was not just a one-time thing, either. When I moved to Washington for my career, the last words my momma said to me before I left her house in Warrenton, North Carolina were "Find you a good church and you will find some great people. I am praying for you, Brenda." I understand now why she spoke those words to me. After leaving, I often reflected on seeing and hearing her pray for others, which she did in the early morning hours and all throughout the day. It was her lifestyle. How many people she must have interceded for? How many lives and hearts and souls she must have changed?

I did not understand all this right away, though. As a young adult Christian, I had a hunger that was not fulfilled. So, I asked God to explain, to show me the meaning of intercession vividly so I could understand the impact of "praying for others." I really wanted to fully comprehend.

And this question was answered! Within weeks of making that request to God, I was moved out of the natural realm and into the spiritual realm, where I received the following vision, or a scene delivered by God to grant me new wisdom and revelation.

I needed to go into a building for some important purpose. I opened the door to the building easily enough, and walked in thinking that I was on the right floor, but quickly learned that I was in the wrong place. So, I turned and walked down some stairs, to catch an elevator down to the bottom floor where I was meant to be. And when I got there, I thought "good I am now on the right floor."

But even when I reached the right floor, there were many hindrances that kept me from getting to the correct room where this important thing was meant to happen.

First, the doorway to the hall had wooden planks nailed all across the door. I had to find something to step on to reach them. With no tools, I attempted to pull out the nails and the planks with my bare hands. Using all my strength, I could not rip out the nails, nor take down the planks. But then it came to me, "With God, all things are possible." (Matthew 19:26) With supernatural help, from having the words of scripture in my mind, I used all the strength in my body, and I was able to remove all the planks and nails from the doorway with my hands. Since they were no longer in my path, I breathed a sigh of relief; surely now I could immediately walk straight through the door, for the way was clear!

But there were more challenges in store. Above the door I had just cleared, water began pouring from the ceiling, and I knew it would make the hallway impassable, drowning out everything. And by now I was mentally exhausted and physically out of breath because of all the hard work I had just done to pull out those nails and planks.

But I had an assignment from God. I had to reach a room on this floor.

I started to look for a bucket to catch the water. Once I found one, I set it down underneath the flowing water. Then I saw that by some miracle, it was enough to contain the downpour. So somehow, through a wonder that should not have been possible for me to achieve, I managed to clean up the water catastrophe. And I was so relieved, thinking I could finally get to the designated room now that I can walk through this door. I felt I had finally made it!

But when I opened the door to the hallway, to my dismay, I was met with another challenge. There was a long hallway ahead of me, stretching and curving into the distance, so far away I could not see the end of it. But I still knew I had to reach the designated room. At this point, I was feeling a distinct pressure, like there was a time I had to be there, and I was so close to missing that time entirely.

So, I set off walking swiftly down that hallway, hoping I could be quick enough to be at the room by some appointed time. I walked for what seemed like miles and miles. I began to wonder what would happen if I could not be there in time...

Finally, I reached the right door and I even said to myself, "I made it!" When I turned the knob, though, it was locked, and I had no key to get in, no idea if knocking would help or even be heard.

I heard voices in the room. At my side, a soft voice from nowhere told me, "The door is locked, but voices mean it is not too late. There is hope as long as there is breath."

This message made clear why I had gone through so many obstacles to get to the room. The people inside needed ministering. And because they were still alive, no matter what they were involved in, it was not too late. There was still hope for them to be delivered.

Then the door opened. (I don't know how it was opened, whether someone on the other side, or if it was supernaturally opened for me.) But what I do know is as

31

soon as I got in the room, I was in the presence of the "voices" I was meant to help.

This vision was very detailed and vivid, but also, it was descriptive in helping me understand intercession. What did I learn? Many things, but first of all, that God is always on time! And likewise, as long as there is breath, there is hope for someone.

Intercession is purposeful, persistent, unswerving work that is selfless on behalf of others. As my vision showed me, we can't be discouraged or stopped by obstacles, distractions, roadblocks, time restraints, and other difficulties that we encounter when we go to minister to others.

I also realized that we must fight spiritually, using prayer, the Word of God, and every fiber within ourselves, to work for the deliverance of others. We cannot give up on anyone. As long as that person has breath, we can still fight for them and there is hope.

In life, someone is always going through something. The correlation, therefore, is that someone should always be interceding for them. We will all face difficulties; we will also know someone, or sometimes many people, who are going through their own difficulties. But God will always see us through, whether we are the one interceding or the one needing intercession.

As my vision was symbolic to physical warfare, intercession is symbolic to spiritual warfare. Think about it. In the vision I just recounted, everything I needed was already available in that place of obstacles even before I arrived. Things I did not even know I would need to complete the journey; God had already provided for me. These included:

1. The door to enter the building
2. Stairs to catch the elevator
3. The elevator to reach the correct floor
4. The stepping-stool to reach the planks nailed over the doorway
5. That more-than-human strength to pull down the nailed planks
6. The bucket to catch the water
7. The strength added in my soul (mind, will, and emotions) to endure an unrelenting journey and a great distance down a long hall
8. The quiet voice at the end of the hall, assuring me that there was still time to aid those in

need of my ministry.

I am reminded of the story of David, who killed a lion and a bear with his own hands. He did not need a weapon, which he did not have anyway. He just needed what God had already blessed him with, his hands. (Consider 1 Samuel 17:34-37.)

Ask yourself, what has God already blessed you with for your own journey? Whatever we need, God has already placed it inside of us, on us, or around us within our reach. Just like everything I needed physically to reach the persons in my vision, God had it there ready for me. He always prepares us for what He calls us to do, which includes equipping us to accomplish His will.

In my case, my journey was to be an obedient servant. My vision reflected this, asking me to overcome all the twists, turns, and obstacles on my way to a designated room, to reach people who were on the brink of destroying their lives.

I encourage you to ask yourself:

1. What are you called to do?
2. Have you encountered dreams which symbolize your purpose?
3. What were you given to overcome the obstacles in your way – both in your dream, and in life?

Reflection

1. Discuss a time you stopped praying for something or someone, but later wished you had persisted.

2. Can you recall an instance where you changed instead of what or who you were praying for? What was learned from that experience?

3. How has uniting in prayer helped you (i.e., prayer partner/prayer line)?

ALIVE FOR THE JOURNEY

Chapter 3

Running From The Truth

As these stories of my life so far have shown, intercession has always played a part in my journey, whether I realized it at the time. Sometimes it was those in my life interceding for me, as when my mother and my elders gave me examples that helped me fast and pray to join the first string of my basketball team, or my mother's intercession which helped me walkway unharmed from a dangerous car trip. But more and more over time, it was me learning what intercession I could offer, such as in the vision of traveling to minister to those in a locked room.

Jesus is the Greatest Intercessor who interceded on our behalf. (See examples from Luke 22:32, Romans 8:34, Hebrews 7:25, and more.) Following His example, I have found that if there is breath, then it is never too late to intercede on behalf of others.

But I didn't fully realize all this right away. As an adult, I came to a very uncomfortable place in my life where it felt as if I was spiritually locked up, all alone in a room in my mind. I was now living in Cincinnati, Ohio, where I had only a few friends and people I knew due to the recent move, again made for my career at the time. It was as if I was holding on to a rope at one end and God was pulling the other end to get my attention, but I was not feeling His movement at all.

During this time, there were so many people who knew me, and even people who did not know me, were compelled to tell me what God was saying about my spiritual journey or what He wanted me to do. Here are four examples that took place around this point in my life.

First, one day I went out to the mailbox to get my mail and the mailman (who I later found out was also a pastor) was standing close by. This was the first time we'd met, so we introduced ourselves cordially and spoke briefly of my move to the area and about finding a church home. And no, I did not visit or join his church! He said to me, "You know, you are called to preach the gospel and maybe even marry a preacher." I thought to myself, *how do you know I am not already preaching the gospel? You don't know anything about me.* I was adamant that he was wrong about his prediction. He didn't even know me. Ironically, my daddy had been a pastor, and my mom was a preacher back when it wasn't popular for women to be preachers. I witnessed the rejection my mom experienced, and I knew I could not have dealt with that kind of unfair treatment gracefully. All of this was holding me back from receiving that truth, which now the mailman was speaking to me.

A second example took place when I returned to North Carolina for a Christmas holiday. Upon entering my mother's home, I was introduced to a new family member I had never met before; he married my cousin. He said, "Nice to meet you, Brenda, you know you have been called to preach the gospel - are you preaching yet?" I abruptly said, "I am not a preacher and I have not been called to preach." He immediately replied, "Young lady, there is a mark on you to preach the gospel, just know that." I dismissed what he said, but like Joseph's father, "I kept the matter in mind". (Genesis 37:11 NIV)

A third example happened when my dear late friend, along with her daughter and niece, visited me in Cincinnati from Washington for two weeks. We had a blast: cooking, eating, going to a theme park, shopping, going to church, etc. As I was driving her to the airport to return home, she looked at me and said, "Brenda, why are you running from your calling? You know God has called you to preach the gospel." I was startled because her words seemed to have come from out of nowhere; during her entire visit we never even mentioned or talked about anything like that. So, I looked at her and said, "God has not called me to preach the gospel and I am tired of hearing this." I dropped her off at the airport, but her words stayed with me: *You know God has called you to preach the gospel.* I rejected what she said to me, even though I could not get those words out of my mind.

Thinking about what my friend had told me, I told God on that same day, which was a Monday: "If you have something for me to do, let me know by 5:00 p.m. Friday. If you don't let me know by then, I am through with this 'being called to preach the gospel thing' because I am tired of hearing people trying to speak that over my life."

Much like Nebuchadnezzar, King of Babylon in the Bible, was troubled by a dream (Book of Daniel, Chapter 4), I was also deeply unsettled in my thoughts that week because of what had been said to me so many times about preaching. People meant to be encouraging, but it always felt more like a bomb dropped in my soul. I didn't have peace all week, nor did I have an appetite for food. In between my uneasiness, I was concentrating on what was going to happen by the deadline I had set for God at the end of the week. (Yes, I realize now, what a presumptuous thing that was!)

5:00 p.m. on Friday evening came and I had not received anything from the Lord. So, I sighed a nervous sigh of relief and said to myself, "I am free from the preaching thing."

Now, the church I attended there in Cincinnati had an all-night prayer that same Friday from 7:00 p.m. until Saturday morning at 7:00 a.m. After some indecision, I decided to attend. After about three hours engaging in a powerful prayer service, I became extremely restless and irritated for no reason. The best thing for me to do, I decided, was to just go home and sleep. So immediately, I exited out the church doors. I made it home, showered and got in bed to just peacefully sleep since I had not rested well in a week, while waiting to hear from God.

As soon as my head hit the pillow, I fell into a deep night vision. I was running in a circle trying to get away from someone who was chasing me. While trying to hide from the person, I saw a building that had a door, so I opened it, ran inside, and closed the door behind me. Shortly after being in the building, with my body shaking, I slowly cracked open the door and peeped out of it, trying to see if it was clear for me to come out to safety away from the chaser. As I peeped out the door, I saw countless women marching together in rows of three, moving straight in one direction. One woman who was on the last row suddenly turned towards me, looked straight in my eyes, and said to me, "BRENDA, STOP RUNNING, YOU CAN'T HIDE. YOU KNOW GOD CALLED YOU TO EVANGELIZE."

I opened my eyes from this vision early that Saturday morning, with tears streaming down my cheeks, feeling as if I was the only person on earth, all alone. As I cried uncontrollably, I told myself, "This vision is not of God; don't receive it, Brenda."

Yes, I was talking to myself. And, yes, I was quite wrong. The next several hours continued to prove it. Evangelistic confirmations of my calling kept coming to me throughout the next 24 hours after that morning vision.

A second confirmation came during a telephone conversation with my girlfriend on the West coast at 6:00 a.m. (PST) that same morning. This call was definitely not to tell her about the dream, but just to hear her voice and talk about her upcoming college graduation. I also imagined myself getting as far away as I could from Ohio, where I had just received this vision. While we were talking about me coming to her graduation in California, she immediately changed the subject and said, "Brenda, why are you running from your calling?" I started crying profusely and said, "Why are you asking me that?" She, without hesitation said, "God placed that in my spirit to say to you." Then, I told her about the vision I had earlier, and she said, "Kearney, you know that is of God." I cried some more and said I didn't believe it was of God, then I hurried to get off the phone with her. At that time, I rejected her words, and through them, rejected God's Word too.

The third confirmation came when a woman who was like a mother-figure to me called around noon and said, "Brenda, I am washing some vegetables, looking out the window and the Lord said He has done something special for you today. What's going on, Brenda?"

I stood there speechless, unable to answer. Then, I cried, and I told her the evangelistic vision I had earlier. She said, "I guess God wants to give you another confirmation." I said to myself, "This is not a confirmation for me. This is not *from* God; this is not *of* God. I do not receive this."

Why was I reacting this way, over and over again? Because I didn't want to be a preacher.

Why was I rejecting this calling in this way? Because I felt that someone was trying to make me be what my parents were…preachers.

Why was I afraid to accept that calling? Because maybe I thought I would lose some friends. Maybe I thought people would not accept me.

Why not me? Maybe I was afraid to come into what I was born to be.

After these happenings early on Saturday, I stayed in bed for the rest of the day, just crying. I also called a sister-girlfriend in South Carolina and told her what transpired within the last 24 hours. In a soft and gentle voice, she asked, "Are you going to tell God no?" Astonished, I asked her, "How do I tell *God* no?" She had no answer, but just breathed a sigh of relief because of my response.

I could not get out of bed even to shower or eat until Sunday morning, when it was time to get dressed for worship service, which I was dreading. I was depleted of every ounce of strength and desire within me.

But I received a fourth confirmation as I walked into the sanctuary with baggy eyes, my rest broken, feeling emotionally and mentally exhausted. I could hear the choir singing, "Yes, Lord, I will say yes to Your will." I started crying again. I told myself, "That song is not for me." But I could not stop crying until the pastor started preaching. As the tears flowed down my cheeks like an overflowing river, I said, "That song is not for me, it is for somebody else." I was still unable to receive – or perhaps, I should say, I still *refused* to receive.

Once upon a time in my life, a time that was continuing into that moment, I was rebellious and I isolated myself to my own will, my own way – and thus, not considering God's Word. I selfishly ignored, refused to receive anything from anyone that I was not ready to do or accept. I dismissed the wisdom of a familiar Scripture as if it was never in the Bible, "For my thoughts are not your thoughts, neither are your ways my ways, saith the Lord" (Isaiah 55:8 KJV).

Whatever I might have said, I was not yet ready to receive His thoughts and ways for my life. So, as the worship service that Sunday continued and became more powerful, I did not budge in my will or my way despite all I had experienced the last day or so.

But, God did not allow me to rest. A fifth confirmation was revealed in the pastor's preaching and message, which was coming from Judges, where Gideon is called to lead Israel back to their covenant relationship (Judges 6:12). As the pastor put it that day, "God called Gideon and He is calling others today. He is calling you today." (Yes, I was thinking...he must be talking to someone in the congregation.) But the pastor continued "Don't be afraid, God will guide you. He has prepared you. The Lord is with you. As the Lord was with Gideon, the Lord is with you."

That was what it took: I softly cried, a dignified cry, and looked up toward the ceiling of the church to heaven, I said humbly, "Yes Lord, I will say yes to Your will."

I couldn't run anymore; I was tired. He had finally won. So, I went home that day knowing, finally, that God had called me. He had given me assurance not to be afraid, for He would guide me, prepare me, and be with me.

Looking back now, it is amazing to me that it took five confirmations to push me out of my will over to submit to His will. Five is the number of grace and grace means favor (See E.W. Ballinger's *Number in Scripture*, Chapter 5, page 135.) I felt then, and still do to this day, that I am unworthy, for Him to consider me as His servant, with all my denials. This is truly Grace. It was imperative for me to know that I was called by God, and not by a human or human means, to preach the Gospel. Thirty-six hours later my whole world changed, and it would never be the same again.

After such an earth-shaking worship service that morning, I went home, took a good nap, ate lunch, and was excited to return to church for the Sunday night service.

There I encountered yet another confirmation, though by now I had been convinced. As soon as I got out of my car to go into the church that night, a mother of the church ran up to me and asked, "Young lady, are you a missionary?" (This denomination called women preachers missionaries.) I looked at her and smiled. Before I could answer her, she said to me,

"There is something about the calling of God that is on your life." I let her finish confirming and encouraging me. Then I boldly and proudly proclaimed to her with confidence and a smile, that yes: I was a preacher with an evangelistic calling.

In the end, I learned much from this experience. God's will is not always easy or what we want to do. However, it all comes down to this: what did God say? What has God prepared for us? What were we born to do?

For me, I learned that day, now I know, that I was born to preach the Gospel, and the foundational scripture that I stand on is: "Apostle Paul said for though I preach the gospel, I have nothing to glory of: for necessity is laid upon me; yea, woe is unto me, if I preach not the gospel!" (1 Corinthians 9:16 KJV)

Various translations of the same verse all emphasize the same ideas: the obligation and necessity of preaching God's Word when you're called to do so.

- I am compelled by God to preach.
- I am obligated to preach.
- Necessity is laid upon me.
- I am under compulsion.
- Obligation is placed on me.

- Preaching is something God told me to do.
- This obligation has been entrusted to me.
- Necessity is imposed upon me.
- Woe if I preach not the gospel.
- Woe is to me, if I do not proclaim the Good News or preach the good news.
- If I don't do it, I am doomed.
- How horrible it will be for me if I don't spread the Good News.
- How terrible it would be for me if I did not preach the gospel.

I experienced just what these various translations describe: Necessity is laid upon me, without excuse, to do what God called me to do. Thinking back now, I am glad I get to do what I was born to do and what the Lord has ordained me to do: to preach the gospel, win souls, and help prepare people for eternity with God.

I am not the only one with a calling. I have witnessed vocations in those around me as well. When my great-nephew was five years old, he said to me, "Aunt Brenda, I was born to make you happy." And you know what? He always makes me happy, and he has done that from an early age, not just by his words but by his actions. He would call me, visit me, give me gifts, and make sure I got invited to every event his parents planned, including out-of-town vacations. If this is his calling, then necessity is laid upon him to make me happy, and I am well pleased. Likewise, necessity is placed upon me to fulfill God's will in winning souls, which brings joy to heaven. (See Luke 15:7 KJV)

I am happy that God entrusted me to lead others into eternal life, and I now want to please God and serve the people He has assigned to me. As stated in the Book of Jeremiah, "Before I formed you in the womb, I knew you (and approved of you as My chosen instrument), And before you were born I consecrated you (to myself as My own); I have appointed you as a prophet to the nations" (Jeremiah 1:5 AMP).

Soon after I finally accepted my calling, I felt I had received a double blessing. Just as I was embarking on an evangelistic journey, I was also relocating from Ohio and starting a new career in South Carolina.

It was tremendous news! But my faith was still being challenged. I wondered if this new journey would lead to blessings, curses, or disappointments.

Reflection

1. Have you noticed any similarities between you and fellow family members related to life events, preferences, gifts/callings, abilities and assignments (natural or spiritual)?

    a. How do/did you feel about it? Note which descriptions may apply: confused, frightened, jealous, unworthy, less capable, relieved, honored, afraid of repeating their mistakes.

    b. What mistakes have you observed in their lives that you may possibly avoid?

2. Is there anything for which you're awaiting confirmation? How long have you been waiting?

3. Name someone who explained something to you that you previously did not understand or believe but now you do.

What did they say?

Chapter 4

Shaken But Not Forsaken

Once all the furniture was packed, loaded onto the moving van, and off to South Carolina, I was so happy. I had a few more days left to finish work at my old job after the moving van pulled out. But finally, my assignment was over in Ohio, my best girlfriend and I would take turns driving the distance of almost nine hours to South Carolina, where I would be starting that new job. I was excited because I was now moving much closer to my family in North Carolina, after living in the Pacific Northwest, the Midwest, and now moving back to the South. Not to mention several of my friends had relocated from Washington to Aiken, South Carolina, so in many ways, it felt like this was the family getting back together.

The day of the drive, my girlfriend and I were both tired since we had worked the day before, but still, we decided to get up early and start our journey to my new home in Aiken. Though I was so tired, I started off driving, and my friend fell asleep.

While traveling on I-75 South, a major interstate through Kentucky, I had been driving for about two hours, when suddenly, I felt a very heavy hand on my left shoulder, shaking me back and forth. It woke me right up because *I had fallen asleep while driving.*

When I realized what had happened, I grew hysterical and started crying profusely. I suddenly realized that while asleep at the wheel, I crossed three lanes of traffic from far right to far left. And I had been completely unaware of it, with no recollection of even falling asleep.

I had lost myself in an unsafe place, surrounded by the danger of big fast trucks and cars on a major interstate where most vehicles were driving 70 or 80 miles per hour. I had been in trouble and wasn't even aware of it. Thank God my life was in the hands of a just

God, whether conscious or not.

I was crying and at the same time, praising God for sparing my life from death. I was thanking God for angels protecting us. I could not stop praising Him.

My friend woke up then and, seeing me horrified but praising God, she asked me what was wrong. Shaken and grateful to God, I told her that I had fallen asleep at the wheel, and per her instructions, I immediately pulled over so she could take the wheel. She drove from that point all the way to Aiken.

Today, thinking back on that story, I am convinced that an angel saved my life. I am reminded of Peter in Acts, "And, behold, the angel of the Lord came upon him, and a light shined in the prison; and **he smote** Peter on the side, and raised him up, saying, Arise up quickly. And his chains fell off from his hands" (Acts 12:7 KJV).

Just like the angel smote Peter on the side, so an angel shook me unmercifully on the shoulder, and in both instances, God woke us up out of sleep in the midst of danger. "For the angel of the Lord is a guard; he surrounds and defends all who fear him" (Psalm 34:7 NLT).

Another scriptural verse that is applicable here

is the story of the shepherd seeking one lost sheep from his flock of a hundred. Here the man leaves the 99 sheep who are safe, going out to seek the one lost sheep until he finds it. Then "When he hath found the lost sheep, he layeth it on his shoulders, rejoicing." (Luke 15:4-5). The shepherd carried the lost sheep to safety.

In my story of falling asleep at the wheel, I was unaware of the danger. The angel used my shoulder to let me know God was carrying me to safety. I thank God that He oversaw the traffic flow that day. He controlled the movement of the traffic on I-75, miraculously holding it back to keep us safe. And because of that, I am Alive for the Journey.

Intercession has happened here as well. Angels, who are ministering spirits, protected me and saved my life. So did the prayers of my mom who always told me, "I am praying for you." Also, the prayers of all those who covered me from across Washington, Ohio, and other places. They all interceded for me for many years before this day, for such a time as this.

When I think of the goodness of God and all that He has done for me, including protecting us from death that day, I am reminded of a quote by Rick Warren, which says: "Grace is when God solves our greatest problem before we even know it is a problem."

That day on I-75, I was safe before I even knew that I was *not* safe. But God! Grace! I am alive for the journey because I was created to withstand, overcome, and survive many challenges for the great work ahead of me, spiritually and naturally.

I made it safely to South Carolina after that major scare, shaken but secure in Him. But new challenges awaited me there, in a new season, a new day, where I began a new job.

Reflection

1. Can you recall a moment in your life when you could not control your situation or outcome, BUT GOD...DID?

2. Have you ever shared that testimony with anyone?

3. Discuss a time you survived an experience that could have killed you.

Chapter 5

The Winning Combination

I had a big surprise the first day I started work at this new job. When I got there, I was looking forward to my new assignment, and to working with the awesome new manager who interviewed and hired me. Unfortunately, on my first day reporting in, I was informed that I had been reassigned to a different manager who I had never met, and to another department doing something I never interviewed for. Worse, there was negative feedback about this manager to whom I'd been reassigned: people said he was not very pleasant, and in fact, he was the worst boss in the department.

After relocating 525 miles, that was the news I received about my new job.

Surprisingly, right from the start of my experiences with my new boss, he was not as bad as I had heard. In fact, the truth is that I am probably writing this book today because this new boss challenged me, perhaps awakening something in me that was lying dormant or that I didn't know I possessed. Before working for him, I had a tremendous fear of writing. Well, working for him shook all that up!

Oftentimes, I had over 200 pages of documents submitted to him, which would take months to finalize for submission. He would always mark them up and send them back for me to correct. He told me once, something along the lines of "There is great potential in you, and I am going to bring it out."

I cried several nights and days while finishing the work I submitted to him. Still, he believed in me and that finally caused me to believe in myself. Now, looking back, I can truly say he was one of the best managers I had in my career. Because he pushed me to excel and helped me to become more polished in my writing. I am not afraid to write anymore. In fact, now I even enjoy writing.

I now understand the saying that "one man's trash can be another man's treasure." This manager may have been someone else's nightmare (and he was my nightmare too sometimes), but he was also a major blessing to me. I learned a lot from him, and he pushed me to excel, not to settle for being mediocre and to strive higher in writing. Ultimately, this manager was a treasure in my life.

But things never stop changing and challenges never stop coming. Otherwise, how would God push us to be better, too?

As I was settling into my quaint new town, enjoying seeing all my friends, finding a new great church family, and visiting my family across Georgia and North Carolina, I received some disappointing news about my health.

After seeing a doctor to look into some health challenges, I was informed that in order to resolve the issue, I needed to have a hysterectomy, and eventually I did. I was very disappointed, and I felt damaged, because at that point in my life, I desired to have children in the future but was realizing that would not be possible for me.

This situation reminded me of a beautiful but

damaged end table I purchased once. I intentionally placed it in certain positions so the "damaged" part would not be seen. The question for me at that point became: how do I keep moving forward without everyone seeing my vulnerability, the "damaged" me? Am I like the end table, that cannot be used fully, but only partially, where part of it must be hidden so the flaws will not be on display?

These days, I also sometimes wonder to myself whether I played a role in my own health issues and the need for a hysterectomy. I am ashamed to admit that as a teenager I boldly declared, "I don't want to give birth or have any children." This is something I came to regret later. Did I contribute to my own health issues? As Proverbs 18:21 (KJV) says, "Death and life are in the power of the tongue."

Words are powerful! What we say, we will get. As a teenager, I spoke death to my womb, and therefore no children would be born to my womb. I often wondered if my words contributed to me not bearing children. We must be careful of the words we say. It took time, but eventually I forgave myself, received forgiveness, and was released. Even today, I feel liberated saying and writing this. Just as the song says, "I am free, thank God

I am free."

But back then when it first happened, my moaning and groaning over being physically childless left me bitter and resentful. I didn't want to be around people who had children, especially during Christmas.

I am not the only one who holds such beliefs, either. I also had a very unpleasant conversation one Christmas with some people whom I love dearly. They told me I would never experience true love, because it only comes from experiencing the love of a child. Oh, did I feel humiliated knowing that I could never give birth to a child! Those words reverberated deeply with an unexplainable hurt and pain. I felt as if someone had ripped out a part of my heart, one that could not be restored or healed. At the time I was thinking *how dare you tell me that, why are you hurting me as if sticking a knife in my heart!*

At the time, I didn't have the strength to tell them that I possessed the greatest love, which is the love of Jesus. Because I "love the Lord thy God with all my heart and with all my soul and with all my mind." (Matthew 22:37 KJV) Now I know that, with children or not, I HAVE THE GREATEST LOVE!

Still, I had a plethora of things to get over from

dealing with the surgery, which I thought defined my womanhood. I dealt with everything from insensitive comments and questions, even to some people thinking no man wants to marry a woman who can't bear children.

One day while reading a book about a woman having a hysterectomy, it was pricked in my heart that even though she was having one part of her body removed, her ministry was not affected. God never allowed this woman's mouth to be silenced. He allowed something that she didn't need to be removed, but still used her mouth to preach the gospel. The beauty of it is her ministry didn't stop, but actually blossomed. The more I read Romans 12:1, I believe God softened my heart even though I was still walking in some bitterness.

Shortly after reading that book, a door was opened for me to attend a church convention with my dear godmother in Milwaukee. I really didn't want to go, but I told myself, think of it like a free week of vacation. So, I attended the event but not with the best spirit, still dwelling on my inability to have children.

Once the conference started on the first day, I planned to attend the individual sessions and the general session. I changed my mind and decided to just sit in the same room rather than attending any individual sessions. My reason was because I had a good seat for the general session, and I didn't want to move.

But next thing I knew, the individual session moved near me where I was sitting. Although I was not part of the session, I overheard the instructor say, "Priscilla and Aquila (Acts 18) were great parents." I thought to myself, *they were not even parents, you are lying.* I, of course, was thinking about biological parents, given everything that I had just experienced with my own health.

But it was as if the instructor had heard my thoughts. Her next words were like an answer directly back to me, as she told the individual session attendees, "Yes, they were parents, they birthed souls into the Kingdom."

Immediately, I began to weep uncontrollably as an inaudible voice inside of me whispered *"Brenda, you are a mother. I have called you to be a great mother - one of the greatest mothers in the world, I have called you to birth souls into the kingdom. Do not ever say you are not a mother. No, I have called you to be a great mother, a mother to many, to birth souls into the kingdom."*

Oh, how I felt purpose and God's love for me, and others!

From that day in Milwaukee onward, I moved forward in my purpose, and my journey was sealed without regrets or feelings of inferiority. I 100% knew God loved me with an everlasting love and had called me to preach the gospel. I knew God didn't care whether I was short or tall, black or brown, educated or uneducated, rich or poor, male or female, young or old, birthed children of my own body or not, from the city or from the country. I recognized the necessity of my evangelistic calling was to help birth sons and daughters into the Kingdom.

My greatest honor in my life is that I was approved by God to work for Him, and it was the beginning of preparation.

After that experience, I began studying and preparing to become a "licensed evangelist" through the Church of God In Christ, and in time I accomplished that goal.

During my early years of ministry, I ministered to many children. I co-started an after-school tutoring and transportation ministry with my dear sister-friend, who is now deceased. My ministry expanded into teaching various classes to students from many age groups and circumstances. I also led and assisted in many other areas of the local churches during my tenure in various states, from Washington and Ohio to South Carolina and too many more to name.

I am reminded that, in order for a flashlight to shine, it must have positive and negative batteries; it must be a combination. I thank God for both the negative circumstances and the positive victories in my life that have propelled me to shine for His glory, a winning combination. Without both the negative and positive, I would not be Alive for the Journey.

In time, I resigned from my job in Aiken, South Carolina and was led, through night dreams, confirmation through the Word, and people of God, to move to Winston-Salem, North Carolina. Thus, the Journey always continues.

Reflection

1. Have you ever been "full of" or "pregnant with purpose?"

      a. To what extent did you carry your purpose?

      b. To what extent did your purpose carry you?

2. Has anyone ever given you an idea and you were inspired to see it through to completion? Please explain!

3. List three ways to encourage childless individuals or couples.

Chapter 6

Committed to the Unknown

One day while I was passing through Winston-Salem for business, I decided to stop. It was a city that I had not visited in over ten years. It was, however, a place continually in my dreams. I felt I would "journey to" Winston-Salem and it would eventually be my next place of abode. Still, I had no family and friends in the city at the time, even though I expected to move there one day.

I actually lived in Winston-Salem and graduated from Winston-Salem State University (WSSU). Three years after graduating from WSSU, I left Winston-Salem and lived in three different states: Washington, Ohio, and South Carolina.

For about a year while living in Aiken, SC, I had this recurring dream of me driving all over and throughout the city of Winston-Salem. In the dream, I was just in my car driving from one place to another.

I felt a strong urge to visit WSSU and there was an unction not to be ashamed to tell people this, even though I didn't know *when* I would go and *where* I would live. All I knew was that I had to confidently tell everyone where I was moving to, and it was not where I was living at the time, in Aiken.

As fate would have it, I was asked the question once and I gave the answer, "I am moving to Winston-Salem." Of course, God was preparing me, even if I did not know it yet. Because when I answered that, I was asked where I would live in the city, and I told my questioner that I still had to find a place. Immediately, I was given the name of a realtor who I recognized as someone I had known when I was attending college there.

When I called the realtor, she remembered me. I informed her that I was moving to Winston-Salem in months (a guess), and I was looking for a 2-bedroom,

2-bath townhouse. And guess what she said, "I got that just for you. I started to rent it, but something never let me rent it." She told me it was mine if I wanted it, and I had to say yes, even without seeing it.

Later, I visited the property along with my dear friend, to give that realtor my deposit. Upon driving through the beautiful neighborhood and seeing the gorgeous homes, I was ecstatic, just smiling and saying, "Look at God." The area was beautifully manicured with different styles of homes, not all the same as cookie-cutters homes.

I pulled into the parking space in front of my soon-to-be-home. As soon as my girlfriend and I opened the doors and stepped out of the car, a little older Caucasian woman came from next door towards us. When I saw the lady, my countenance changed from a smile to an unfriendly *don't mess with me, older white lady, because I am tired of dealing with racism.* Oh, I was sure she didn't want me as her neighbor because I am black. I had my guard up like steel bars around a jail before she even opened her mouth. To my surprise, this frail, gentle woman walked over to me with a warm smile and asked with excitement if I was moving next door to her. With some reservation I said yes, and steeled myself to hear her next words, ready to hear something harsh or upsetting.

But what did this complete sweet stranger gently say? "I have been praying for you for a year. I asked God to send me a neighbor, a person, to this place next to me. I asked specifically for someone who loved Him more than anything, a person who not just attends church by being a bench member, but one who serves God with everything, every fiber within them."

At this point I fell on the pavement, crying tears of joy, knowing that God sent me to that place, that address, that neighborhood because of the intercession of a dear older godly lady who did not know me yet and had never met me before.

Intercessory prayer landed me a new home. It was amazing that this woman had been praying for me for a year and at the same time during that year, I had dreamed many recurring dreams about being in Winston-Salem. Look at God. Intercession works!

She said, "Brenda, just know you are the one I have been praying for a year and I am thrilled to have you as my neighbor."

The lessons in this chapter could be summarized like this:

- Intercession is not based on race or whether we know the person or not. My new neighbor's prayer was for a Godly person as a neighbor, and when God answered her prayers, she got to witness it.
- Don't be biased based on past experiences. Be open to the blessings of God.
- Intercession is both for people we know and those we don't know. So, the right answer can be received for both. In my case I saw it both:
1. for my new neighbor, whose intercession resulted in her receiving a Godly neighbor.
2. for me, since in God's timing, I moved to the right city, the right community, and the right condo next to the right neighbor.

Oh, how wonderful it is to experience God's confirmation and know you are in His perfect will!

Little did I know that this sweet older neighbor who was praying for me before I ever met her, would later intercede for me in a serious challenge.

Reflection

1. Do you believe I spoke my new residence into existence by continuing to speak the will of God in expectation?

How does Romans 8:28 fit in this discussion?

2. Just as I am sharing my story, consider sharing yours by using a daily journal to chronicle YOUR life's events.

3. Have your negative expectations ever influenced your responses to other people?

   a. In Chapter 5, we see a negative report about a manager. What do you perceive was my actual experience?

b. In Chapter 6, we read a negative expectation of a neighbor, based on prior experiences. What do you perceive was my actual encounter?

Chapter 7

Not Unto Death

Once I had settled into my beautiful condo with the greatest peace, decorating my new home and looking for a church home became my focus. I felt peace because I knew that God knew I loved Him with all my heart, soul and mind. I was convinced that He knew whatever He said do, I would do. If He said go, I would go. I felt God knew He could trust me because I gave up my livelihood to follow His voice, not knowing how I would survive in Winston-Salem where He directed me to go. Was it foolishness or faith? I know which one I think it was. I was obsessed with a Godly reverence for obedience.

After being in Winston-Salem for approximately two years, I did what I would describe as "home missions" for one of the local hospitals. I was the Community Volunteer Director, a part-time paid position, for a program that assisted the disabled and older adults with some necessities of life. A year before moving to Winston-Salem, I started having dreams of driving all over the city. In confirmation of this dream, my new position had me driving all over the city visiting residents' homes to assess their needs and then get assistance from churches, agencies, or individual donations to help meet those needs. This position proved to be challenging at times. One day while verifying an address, I had to visit the home of a white guy who refused to acknowledge he lived on MLK Street, named after Martin Luther King, Jr. He cursed the street and said he would always use the prior name of the street simply because the current name was after a black man. Despite his cursing, he was blessed with help also. I used grace, the same way God always did for me.

While working in that job, I had a dream one night where I was in the midst of many angels. Angels were coming at me in all directions. I was reaching towards them over my head, in front of me, and even behind me. Then, there was one angel suddenly affixed to the left side of my body, and that was the end of the dream.

As soon as I opened my eyes, I said, "Oh my God, my body is going to be attacked but God has assigned angels, ministering spirits, to me." I immediately started studying scriptures about angels, including these:

Matthew 4:11 (KJV) "Then the devil leaveth him, and, behold, angels came and ministered unto him."

Psalm 91:11 (AMP) " For He will command His angels in regard to you, to protect and defend and guard you in all your ways (of obedience and service)."

Psalm 34:7 (KJV) "The angel of the Lord encampeth round about them that fear him and delivereth them."

Exodus 23:20 (NIV) "See, I am sending an angel ahead of you to guard you along the way and to bring you to the place I have prepared."

A few months later, I was sporting a pretty new hairstyle, and I picked up a mirror to see my hair from a different angle. I felt the new style was beautiful in the front. However, in the back, the mirror revealed something startling that I wasn't glad to see…a suspicious-looking lump on my neckline.

I was working part-time at a medical facility, without medical insurance, but I was informed by a health professional there that I needed to go see a doctor. A few days later, I scheduled an appointment with a doctor I never visited before to check out the lump. When I chose the doctor, I realized he and his wife, who was also a doctor, were in the practice together, which I thought was amazing. I was not referred to this doctor, I just randomly picked a name out of the phone book – a choice I would soon discover was more than a random pick. As so many things in my life have been, I discovered it was led by God.

Upon arriving at this doctor's office, I was received by an extremely friendly staff member, and within minutes, I was escorted to the examination room. A lively, smiling doctor with a distinct accent walked in and said, "Hi, Bren-dar, nice to meet you. I hear you found a lump on your neckline."

Immediately he looked at the lump, saying if there was something visible on the outside, then there might be something on the inside. I had to wonder, what does he mean? After getting bloodwork and other tests performed in the office, he called his wife in to also look at the lump. I was so amazed that this doctor, on my very first visit to him would spend over an hour with me, treating me as if I was special or one of his family members. I kept forgetting I am special, for I am a daughter of King Jesus (Romans 8:16-17). A beloved friend often reminded me of this.

Some memories of this time are fuzzy, but I do remember this wonderful doctor stated I needed to get a mammogram immediately. He had his office call to schedule my mammogram right away at another location, which I had within weeks. When those results came back, they reported "suspicious calcifications." I was then referred to get a biopsy, and when that was done, there was nothing more to do but wait.

The period of waiting for the biopsy results was painful with the anxiety of possibly being diagnosed with cancer the same way as my older brother, who had died at 39 years of age from brain cancer. And here I was, also 39 years of age. My mind was echoing the same thoughts and prayers I had years ago while driving those dangerous winding mountain roads in Washington: I didn't want my mother to experience yet another unbearable pain or loss.

A second reason for not wanting to hear the word "cancer" was because my heart was set on an upcoming, once-in-a-lifetime trip to Israel, the Holy Land, and Rome, which would take place in just three months. This 12-day trip was a sudden opportunity which required I pay $3,000 within 30 days to cover the cost of airfare, lodgings, and other incidentals. I did not really have the money when I first learned about this opportunity because I was working part time and barely making it. I was living by faith for food, shelter, car repairs, etc. But, as more proof of God still working miracles, He had provided me with the money for the trip. When I'd learned about the chance to go on this trip, I sent letters to family and friends asking them for donations to support this needed spiritual journey. Little did I know what a journey this would be. Within 20 days, I had received over $3,000 to pay for my entire trip. I was rejoicing and singing "I am going to the Holy Land!" So, in one moment I had pure happiness at the thought of visiting these holy places, and then in the next moment I was wondering whether I might have cancer and would not be able to go.

Finally, late one evening when I was all alone, I received a call from the doctor saying the results had come back and, they were positive. In other words, I had breast cancer. What a way and what a time to tell someone that they have cancer! Sitting there, I stared quietly at the walls and the ceiling with many thoughts, some good and some bad. Then I stood up, looked out the kitchen window, and wiped the tears away.

At first, the natural me wanted to think the worst. But, my mind immediately reflected on the dream I had of all those angels coming to me, and one that was attached to my left side. And yes, the cancer had been diagnosed on my left side. So, I held firm to my belief knowing God had given me angels who would minister to me, help me, protect me and order my steps in the time of need, in any adverse situation.

I shared the diagnosis with my family, friends, co-workers, and some church members. I gathered my mom and all my siblings together to share the news, since I knew that my mom would not take it well, having already lost a son to cancer. Unable to bear it, her eyes looked as if they were popping out of her head, and she ran out of the room to cry so that I would not see her tears and pain. She knew how much I loved her and never wanted to give her any pain.

Within a week of receiving the diagnosis, I contacted a surgeon and was referred for an appointment. The appointment was a few weeks after the diagnosis, and I was told that the surgeon did not have a friendly personality. I reminded them that I was not looking for a best friend: I was looking for a great surgeon.

Between the diagnosis and visiting my new surgeon, I had a dream of seeing a black doctor from Montgomery, Alabama. In this dream he was examining me, and I was repeating the words, "faith & fear tactics." End of dream! Within a week or so after that dream, my co-worker who was a practicing Buddhist gave me a book, wrapped in a brown paper bag that hid the title. Since I was getting ready to go to lunch and the library was next door, I decided to go see what the book was about and if I liked it, then I would read it. As I started reading, I saw specific words in the book that reminded me of the dream. The more I read, the book seemed familiar. Then, I was prompted to take the brown paper covering off the book to see the title. It was about black women and breast cancer. So, I started reading again, and the second prompt was to see who the author was. Believe it or not, the author was a black doctor from Alabama!

The book was giving pointers and things to say, questions to ask, when seeing your doctor after diagnosis. The author, a treating physician, disclosed that some doctors may not treat others the way they would treat family members. His book gave me valuable information which was the ammunition I needed to make the best choices regarding my diagnosis and treatment. This book was inspirational and encouraging. It was like a bright light, as if Jesus was holding my hand and leading me to the next step.

I felt peace just knowing I was not alone. I cried tears of joy. God will reach us with whatever and whoever is needed. I was forever grateful to my former co-worker, the Buddhist. We can't limit who God will use!

The weeks passed quickly until it was time for me to go visit the surgeon. As I entered the treatment room, I saw about five people. I was left thinking, why all these people? But eventually everyone was introduced, from the surgeon to social worker, maybe a minister and two others, though I remember I came to the appointment alone. After discussing my options, we agreed on a lumpectomy. The surgery was scheduled for a date in July 1995.

I was prepared for the meeting with the right questions, thanks to Dr. Johnson of Alabama who wrote that book I'd been given. The surgeon in Winston-Salem told me, "Young lady, you have done your homework." I started to tell him God did it for me, using Dr. Johnson and my co-worker. I then changed the subject and asked if I would be able to still go on a planned trip the 1st week of September. He answered, "No, because you will be in treatment."

Hearing that, I sobbed right then and there. I certainly cried more over not being able to go on my trip than the news of having cancer. You might wonder: What was I thinking? Did I have my priorities in the right place? Well, time would tell.

After pre-ops were completed, it was finally surgery day. The morning of the lumpectomy I was awakened at 3:00 a.m. crying again, but a sense of inner peace impressed upon me to open my Bible and I did. I opened it to John 11:4 (NIV), which teaches us: "This sickness will not end in death. No, it is for God's glory so that God's Son may be glorified through it." The scripture comforted me and the reason for my tears shifted from *not being sure of the outcome* to *it is going to be all right, and I will not die from this.*

At this point, I had a peace that passed all understanding. What little fear remained, and that was trying to cripple me, was replaced with a mighty faith. I felt like a little girl grinning and skipping down the street to meet my dear friend when I was a child. I was abundantly joyful, for I realized I had just had an encounter with Jesus.

I love being alive for the Journey, and I was grateful to be alive for this journey!

On the way to the hospital that morning, my family witnessed a different Brenda than the one they had seen the night before. I was also met at the hospital by many loved ones, family, and friends from across North Carolina, South Carolina, and Georgia. What a heartening group to see!

Prior to the surgery, I told the doctor I wanted to sign a paper authorizing a mastectomy instead of a lumpectomy if he saw additional cancer once he started. So, the night after the surgery, when the doctor visited me, I asked, "Did you get it all?" The doctor's reply was that we would talk when I came to the office.

I knew it meant the doctor did not get all the cancer out.

Two weeks later, I had my follow-up office visit and was told cancer was found *under* cancer during the surgery. The doctor informed me it appeared to be cancer, but he wanted to make sure and send it off for testing. He stated he didn't want to give me a mastectomy if it wasn't necessary. Based on the new test results, I was scheduled for another surgery, this time a mastectomy two weeks later in August 1995. So, I had that surgery, and everything went well. During this period, I had precious friends who not only came to see about me, but also stayed to take care of me to relieve my devoted family and show me support. They traveled from six different states: Washington, Ohio, Pennsylvania, Illinois, the Carolinas, and Georgia. They all came at their own expense to be a blessing to me.

One of my best friends, who was like a sister to me, was so devastated and heartbroken over what I was going through that she could not bear to come see me in person. Even so, she called daily and supported me in many ways.

Even after the 2nd surgery, the mastectomy, I was not moved by these supposedly challenging misfortunes because I had received a Word from the Lord, telling me,

"This sickness is not unto death…" I considered this my marching orders, regardless of the stage or size of the cancer they found. No, I was not getting ready to die – not me! We either believe God or man, and I chose to believe God. Whose report are you going to believe?

Still, a few weeks later, I was approaching another appointment that I was dreading. I had to meet with the oncologist to find out when I would start chemo. I did not want to take chemo, because I had seen how it affected my dear friend who took chemo for a year. This was many, many years ago by that point, but I would drive her to some of her appointments and witness how sick she was afterwards. Sometimes she would even throw up on the way to the appointment. Because of supporting her during her ordeal, I didn't want to travel that road.

On the other hand, I had a boss who would come to work, leave, and go take chemo, then return to work. He made it seem so easy! Why is it that we dwell on the worst scenario or use it as an example most of the time?

The night before visiting the oncologist, I was very quiet and didn't feel like talking to anyone. I drifted off to sleep earlier than usual and woke up at exactly

3:00 a.m. I began to pray the scripture of Matthew 26:39 (KJV) - Jesus said, "O my Father, if it be possible, let this cup pass from me: nevertheless, not as I will, but as thou wilt." Of course, Jesus was talking about the cup of death, from dying on the cross. But, I begin to call out to the Lord.

I said, "Lord, if it be possible, let this cup of chemo pass from me: nevertheless, not as I will, but as thou wilt." I cried out to the Lord for hours, from 3:00 a.m. until 10:00 a.m., which was the time of my appointment. My awesome brother drove an hour to come take me to the doctor and I had very few words with him because I was yet praying: *If it be possible, let the cup of chemo pass from me.*

I arrived at the doctor's office to meet with the oncologist. As soon as I checked in, a nurse came to get me and showed me the area I would be taking chemo in, but I was still praying, "Lord, if it be possible let the cup of chemo pass from me." I entered the examination room, and the oncologist came in. He said hello and then said, "Brenda, if I didn't see your paperwork and see your body, I wouldn't know you had cancer." He then told me "There are 5 factors that we use to determine if a person should have chemo. You only have one factor, so we are not recommending chemo for you. You will not have to take this treatment."

I rose from the examination table, looked to heaven, and said, "Thank you Jesus! Thank you, Jesus, for allowing the cup of chemo to pass from me."

The oncologist said, "It was a miracle that the radiologist caught it because it was very small." In fact, the office staff were so impressed that they looked back at my records to see who made the miraculous discovery. But God! I didn't have to take chemo, radiation, and any pills. Oh, what a day of rejoicing! *I am alive for the journey!*

Are you wondering about the Israel trip that I was told I could not take because of my upcoming treatment? A week before the trip was supposed to begin, upon going to the doctor for post follow-up, I asked the surgeon again about me going to Israel now. He said, "I don't remember saying don't go; you are released to go." He didn't remember saying it, but I remembered because I was so devastated by even the possibility.

So again, whose report will you believe? I know it was of God for me to go, so I never gave up on His promise to me.

So now, I was released to go, medically, but I did

not have a passport and the trip was in seven days.

While I was out of town recuperating, visiting my mom in my small hometown of Warrenton, North Carolina, I felt urged to go to my congresswoman there and apply for my first-ever passport on that Thursday morning. And guess what: my passport was delivered to me Monday morning in Winston-Salem, North Carolina. Look at God! *I am alive for the journey, and I flew to Israel just as God had promised me.*

We must stand on God's Word.

Remember:
- I was given angels to protect me before I was attacked with cancer.
- I was given the Word to stand on, in the midst of everything. (John 11:4 NIV) "This sickness will not end in death. No, it is for God's glory so that God's Son may be glorified through it." (Mathew 26:39 KJV) "O my father, if it be possible, let this cup pass from me: neverthless not as I will, but as thou wilt."
- I was given a book with pertinent information regarding choices, diagnosis, and treatment

resources for black women.

- My dear co-worker, a practicing Buddhist, sowed into my life by giving me this book as I journeyed through cancer. She was very compassionate and provided me with a gift to help me during my affliction. The book was excellent in answering questions that I had and how to approach different steps, ministering to me tremendously as a Black woman dealing with cancer. I was provoked to be proactive in caring about my health, not just sitting back, and waiting. The book was like God was holding my hands, talking to me, giving me questions to ask, and things to accept and not accept as a black woman.

From these examples, we can see no one human person has the answer. It is God who has all the answers, and He uses different methods and different people to get us what we need. "For my thoughts are not your thoughts, neither or your ways my ways, saith the Lord" (Isaiah 55:8 KJV).

Maybe some of us have missed some blessings – or jobs, resources, connections, even spouses – because we discriminate against who we would receive from and who we would not. In our flesh and its weaknesses, we decide who has a Word for us.

Now. Sometimes things come to test us, make us doubt, but God's Word doesn't change. Situations may change, but our faith shouldn't change. As Jesus told Simon Peter, "Satan hath desired to have you, that he may sift you as wheat. But I have prayed for thee, that thy faith fail not…" (Luke 22:31-32 KJV).

In the midst of everything, I didn't lose my faith. Cancer was removed, controlled, contained, and cured. As my current pastor, Bishop James C. Hash, says, "Satan doesn't want us, he wants our faith." I did not let my faith fail me. Intercession was happening for me all over the world, both through those I knew and those I did not know.

And that, I know now, is why *I am Alive for the Journey.*

Reflection

1. Discuss your experiences, if any, that you may have had with angels.

2. Explain how you will do the research to your challenging situation.

3. How can we be comforted and confident in an uncomfortable situation?

Chapter 8

Blessed To Be A Blessing
- Surrendering All

My motto of *I am Alive for the Journey* is not just about me, but about what I was born to do. I was born to be a survivor, so I could be a blessing to others.

I am reminded of my first or second open vision, a scene from God when your eyes are wide open and God shows you a picture exclusively for you, no one else. I remember I was in the choir, singing and clapping. In a flash, the vision came, and I saw my precious girlfriend glowing and smiling with her hair flowing and her stomach enlarged with child. I remember I stopped clapping, stared for a few moments, then regained my composure and returned to clapping. It was amazing because she had been married for five years and they (she & her husband) didn't have children yet, nor had she announced she was pregnant. As one of her best friends, I knew that she would have told me if she was pregnant.

So, I telephoned this friend that night and told her the vision I had of her being pregnant. She calmly asked her husband to get on this call and I shared the vision with him also. She said, jokingly, "The prophetess has spoken but I am not pregnant yet, but we are still believing God." My sentiments were the same as Amos 7:14 CEV: "I am not a prophet! And I wasn't trained to be a prophet..." I am just a servant of God, being about my Father's business.

Within a month of me sharing that revelation with them, I received a call from this girlfriend, where she screamed, "Prophetess, Aunt Bren, I am pregnant!" And per the doctor, the week of conception was the week she received the phone call from me.

I saw my friend pregnant in the spiritual realm before she became pregnant in the natural. Over the years, I realized that God allowed me to see the process of birthing in the spiritual & natural because he was preparing me to birth children in the spiritual throughout the world. Ministry travels have taken me from the USA to Mexico, Nepal, the Philippines, Belize, Nigeria, Benin, Togo, South Africa, Kenya, and more. As I was extremely happy for my girlfriend and her pregnancy, so God made me extremely happy to do His will in His way! I had to be patient with the process.

I am humbled God has birthed sacrificial love in me for both believers and non-believers of Christ, naturally and spiritually, as indicated in some of the following stories.

Once upon a time some of my dear friends, with little children, were displaced. My heart was moved to assure that the school-age children had stability until their parents' situation changed. Therefore, I allowed the family to move into my home at no charge, for a month or two, and I stayed with a friend during that time. I sacrificed my comfort for them to be comfortable. This is sacrificial love that shows itself in action, by surrendering all. That's what Jesus did!

Another night after church, I drove my girlfriend home about 9:00 p.m. I noticed that she was waiting for me to drive away before she entered her house. The same thing happened the second night. That bothered me, so I blew the horn and asked why she wasn't going into the house, and then she cried while confessing to me she didn't have lights. I took her to my home, and I think she stayed with me for about 8 months. This is sacrificial love: when you see a need, if you can, meet that need, surrendering all.

There was an older childless couple...the husband lived in their home and the wife was in a nursing home. Since they had no family in the area, I would buy food for the husband, cook his breakfast, and clean his place. I then visited the wife at her nursing home, combed her hair, read to her, and tidied up her room. Sacrificial love! Surrendering All!

A young college student I had known for only two weeks at the time was hospitalized with throat cancer around Thanksgiving. All her friends were leaving campus to go home for the holidays, and she was going to be alone on Thanksgiving Day. She didn't have family in the city. I placed myself in her position and knew if it were me, I would want someone with me. Therefore, I canceled Thanksgiving with my own family, stayed all day and night in the hospital with her, and fasted 24 hours on Thanksgiving Day for her health, without eating or drinking anything. All this was for *love thy neighbor as thyself, surrendering all.*

For the last 34 years, I have prayed daily for boys and girls throughout the world who are spiritually hungry, physically sick, hungry, and homeless, lonely, abandoned and rejected, orphans, or emotionally challenged. A recent revelation allowed me to realize how many of them don't have spiritual or natural influences to support them, love them, and pray and intercede for them. My assignment over 34 years ago was to pray for this group as if they were my own children or family members. I am standing in the gap for the people known and unknown to me but known to God. In my heart God gave me these children, and "Children are a gift from the Lord, they are a reward from him" (Psalm 127:3 NLT).

And those are far from the only stories I could tell. One time, I was invited on a 7-day trip to Montego Bay, Jamaica, with all expenses paid for: airfare, hotel, and food. This trip was sponsored by a tourism organization out of Jamaica and intended to introduce U.S. companies to various amenities, resources, and opportunities to have conferences and events in Jamaica. I was traveling with a group of about twenty people from all over the country. The last night there, a party was given for us by some dignitaries of Montego Bay.

I was sitting alone on the couch embracing the love and energy in the room. It was as if everyone else was mingling, passing out business cards, trying to meet the who's who. Suddenly, a young lady came over to me and said, "There is something special about you, tell me about you." I smiled at her. I told her I was an evangelist from North Carolina, and my first love was to pray daily for other people's children, who are my heartbeat. She seemed impressed and wanted to know when I was flying back home. I informed her, the next day around 4 p.m. She said, "I am a teacher, and how perfect is the timing. I am off tomorrow because it is a holiday, and I would love to spend time with you." I said great, so she picked me up the next morning around 7:30 a.m. I didn't even know what I was saying *great* to, but God did. My steps were ordered by the Lord to get chosen to go on the trip and now to spend a day with destiny in my last hours in Montego Bay.

We first went to her beautiful house on the mountaintop overlooking the ocean to retrieve something she had forgotten. I immediately took notice of her family pictures and saw a world-renowned dignitary! When asked about the dignitary, she said, "He is my first cousin." Wow! Even though I was impressed, I did not get sidetracked, but stayed focused on our mission.

We then got back into the car, and she first drove us to a house that was used as a shelter for children aged 6 years and under. I got out of the car with a humble spirit and immediately asked her to open her trunk, where my suitcase was. She opened the trunk; I quickly unzipped my suitcase and grabbed my camera. As soon as I touched the camera, the inner voice told me, *Leave that camera where it is, in your suitcase in the trunk. This is not show and tell, this is ministry time.* Tears now streaming, I repented, and we entered the home. There I was able to hold the children, and to read, play games with, and pray for them. Sacrificial love!

Next, we journeyed to an orphanage. Upon entering the building, we were given a tour. The most heartbreaking part was to see beds stacked upon beds, probably 20 or 30 in a room. From one perspective, it was sad because those beds represented children without the presence of a parent. On the flip side, the beds represented love, and I was thankful that someone cared enough to provide a place for the children. Then I prayed for the entire orphanage – the staff, the children, and the needs of both. I prayed that God would have the right people working with the children, to love them and not hurt them. I also prayed that they all would receive love without conditions, that they would all have food to eat and clothes to wear.

As we continued to walk through the place, I saw one room that had wrinkled clothes galore, piled high and wide. I was informed these were the kids' clothes. They didn't have their own specific clothing. Everybody wore clothes from the same pile, whatever was cleaned for that day. Tears like a mighty river flowed from my eyes. I began to intercede for God's intervention for more than enough to meet all their needs. Sacrificial love!

Then off we went to the next place, which I learned was a prison for male offenders who were 18 years of age and under. My kindhearted host and I were escorted in with guards. Once inside, I was introduced to the inmates and chatted with them. Then, I taught a lesson on forgiveness which led many in the room to receive Christ. Surrendering All!

Finally, we traveled to a place for adults with physical challenges, some mobile and some not. Some could talk and some couldn't. Some could hear and see, while some couldn't. Some had all their limbs, and some didn't. I was able to personally pray God's mercy, protection, blessings, and healing upon all. I prayed that the love of God be upon all staff and those they served.

The night before at the send-off party with the dignitaries, everyone else was mingling, passing out business cards, while I was quietly praying about children in Jamaica and God connected me with the who's who. This connection led me to meet some unknown kids, unknown to me but not to God, for whom I'd interceded for over 34 years.

You are probably thinking, "Brenda was crazy to trust a total stranger alone, and she didn't even know the lady." And you are right, at least for part of that. I didn't know her, but God did. What I had been praying for many years over children was manifested in Jamaica by God's divine timing, and His chosen vessel, my host for that day.

As these different stories show, I am compelled to have the love and compassion of Jesus and to win souls to Christ. I intercede for many, the ones I know and don't know, the ones who have people covering for them and the ones who don't.

"Blessed be God, even the Father of our Lord Jesus Christ, the Father of mercies, and the God of all comfort. Who comforteth us in all our tribulation, that

we may be able to comfort them which are in any trouble, by the comfort wherewith we ourselves are comforted by God." (2 Cor 1:3-4 KJV)

All of these are examples of what I gave freely to other people, as these same gifts were freely given to me by God. As a person acquainted with rejections, disappointments, sickness, pain, near-death experiences, deaths of loved ones, childlessness, homelessness, and more, I knew that God had comforted me in them all. I now know I am able to boldly comfort countless others, not only in prayer, but in love also. Interceding limitlessly, this is a love that shows itself in action, which is sacrificial love, surrendering all, withholding nothing like the song written by William McDowell.

> *Withholding Nothing,*
> *I surrender all to you.*
> *Everything I give to you.*
> *Withholding nothing,*
> *Withholding nothing.*

And I believe, this is the reason I am Alive for the Journey. I Am Blessed To Be A Blessing.

"And I will make of thee a great nation, and I will bless thee, and make thy name great; and thou shalt be a blessing." (Genesis 12:2 KJV)

Reflection

1. How can you discern the differences between an observation and an assignment?

2. Think of difficult moments God has brought you through. How is your purpose related to those moments?

3. What are you willing to sacrifice for others?

A native of North Carolina, Reverend Brenda A. Kearney is a yielded servant, divinely commissioned to impact people of all ages and all walks of life. She is an ordained minister, licensed evangelist, teacher, administrator, servant leader, and trainer.

Reverend Kearney ministers in worship services, seminars, and conferences for women, youth and singles. Her ministerial giftings have taken her throughout the United States and across Africa, where she has visited South Africa, Nigeria, Togo, Benin, Kenya. Given her heart for missions, she has also traveled to Nepal, the Philippines, Belize, Jamaica, and Mexico. She feels compelled to share the gospel and win others to Christ.

She earned a Bachelor of Science in Business Education from Winston-Salem State University and a Master of Divinity from Shaw University Divinity School.

In addition to being involved in the community and serving

on various boards, she also enjoys traveling, shopping, reading, journaling, fishing, and boating. Her love walk extends into her leisure time as she appreciates the art of communicating and compassionately listening to the life experiences of people from all walks of life.

Printed in the USA
CPSIA information can be obtained
at www.ICGtesting.com
LVHW022313080524
779242LV00017B/331